# The Re-Up:
Embracing Life's Most Powerful Season

A Guide to Reclaiming Your Purpose, Power, and Passion

---

Tia Rochelle

The Re-Up: Embracing Life's Most Powerful Season
Copyright © 2024 by Tia Rochelle

All rights reserved. No part of this book may be reproduced or transmitted in any form or by any means without written permission from the author.

ISBN: 979-8-9920972-0-7
Published by: SIP Publications, LLC
https://www.thejuniorauthors.com/sip-publications-llc.html#/
Printed in the United States of America

Edited by: Tia Rochelle
Cover Art: 5.13 Graphics & Media LLC

## Dedication

**A Love Letter to Tia**

Dear Tia,

I love you deeply, but it's time to do the work. You, who have weathered countless storms, stood tall in the face of life's fiercest battles, and who, even when weary, still found the strength to rise. I am here to tell you—this is your time. No more merely existing, no more giving what you no longer have to give. You deserve so much more, and today, you stand ready to reclaim it all.

You are at rock bottom, yes, but you are also at the doorstep of something breathtaking, something powerful and sacred—a rebirth into the life you've always deserved. It's time to promise yourself, once and for all, to show up fully in the mirror, unfiltered, vulnerable, and real, and to love the beautiful soul staring back with all the grace and kindness she deserves.

I am dedicating this book to you—the woman you've been, the woman you are, and the woman you are yet to become. As my shero, Dr. Iyanla Vanzant, says, "It's time to do the work, beloved." Bare-faced, 10-toes down, all in. You must embrace the woman you're called to be. Feel all your feelings. Do whatever it takes to become the best version of you.

In the next three months—one quarter—we will rebuild: mind, body, spirit, and soul. I will stand in the gap for you. I will honor your journey, nurture your dreams, and fight fiercely for your peace. You will no longer be the one left behind; instead, you will be the one leading, the one shining, the one deeply connected to herself and her purpose. You deserve to stand boldly in this world, to fill every room with the fullness of your light, and to claim every blessing that has been waiting for you.

And I promise you this: we will walk every step with courage, with love, and with an unshakeable belief in all that is still possible—toward a life overflowing with purpose, power, and passion.

With all my love,
Tia

## TABLE OF CONTENTS

Introduction ............................................................... 1

Setting the Stage ....................................................... 3

The Butterfly's Metamorphosis ............................. 7

The Eagle's Rebirth ................................................ 9

Re-negotiate ......................................................... 12

Re-Emerge ............................................................ 50

The Contract ........................................................ 62

## Re-Up:

To re-enlist or re-negotiate a contract.

## Introduction

This is my testimony—a raw account of hitting rock bottom, standing in the gap for myself, and deciding to reclaim the life I want. My journey to "re-up" has been a season of transformation and rebirth. At 41, I feel as if I've lived ten lifetimes. I've been a wife and mother since the tender age of 18 and working full-time since I was 14. Now, as a business owner in my 40s, the emotional and mental demands have pushed me to my limits. I woke up one day feeling so empty and disconnected that I wanted to walk away from it all—home, family, business, life.

In my exhaustion, I sought refuge in San Diego with my sister, feeling the desperate need for soul care. I wanted nothing more than to sit alone in a dark room. I was overwhelmed, underappreciated, overworked, and undervalued. I call this "The Over-Unders." It was here, at my lowest, that I finally let myself release everything, breaking open and allowing myself to articulate the burden I was carrying.

I felt like a butterfly in the painful cocoon of transformation or an eagle going through the rebirth process. Both transformations are physically and spiritually demanding, requiring the shedding of what no longer serves and the regrowth of something stronger. This was my metamorphosis—a process of letting go, rebuilding, and trusting that God is guiding me into a new, powerful chapter of life.

In that moment, I understood that I must show kindness to myself, especially in the tender places of my brokenness. This journey isn't just for me; it's for every woman who feels lost, stuck, or uncertain. Together, we're going to "re-up"—to reclaim our purpose, power, and passion, and to renew our contract with ourselves.

## *Setting the Stage for Transformation*

There comes a point in life when burnout, disconnection, and the loss of identity signal a profound need for rebirth. These are not just fleeting moments of stress or fatigue; they are deep soul cries, begging us to pause, reflect, and listen. For me, this wasn't just a crisis—it was a call to come home to myself. After years of constantly showing up for others, I was empty. I had spent so much time pouring into roles, titles, and responsibilities that I had lost touch with who I was beyond them.

In this moment of reckoning, I could no longer ignore the symptoms. Burnout showed up as relentless exhaustion, an inability to find joy in the things I once loved, and a creeping sense of resentment toward even the simplest demands of life. Disconnection left me feeling like a stranger in my own life. I was so used to "doing" that I had forgotten how to simply "be." I was surrounded by people and obligations, yet I felt profoundly alone. My identity had blurred under layers of expectations, responsibilities, and obligations.

This season of my life illuminated something I call "The Over-Unders."

## The Over-Unders

"The Over-Unders" are where I found myself—a place of intense imbalance and inner conflict. It's a state of being in which we are stretched too thin yet feel unappreciated for all we do; a place where we are overextended, but under-acknowledged. Here's what it looked like for me, and perhaps it will resonate with you too:

- **Overwhelmed:** Life had piled on so many demands that I felt buried beneath them. Even small tasks became heavy burdens, and I felt like I was constantly fighting to keep my head above water.

- **Underappreciated:** I poured so much of myself into my roles as a mother, wife, and entrepreneur, yet it often felt like no one truly saw the sacrifices I was making. It was as if my efforts were invisible, unvalued, and taken for granted.

- **Overworked:** My life had become a never-ending cycle of tasks and responsibilities. I worked tirelessly, driven by a sense of duty, but there was no longer any joy in the work. I was on autopilot, moving through the motions without purpose or passion.

- **Undervalued:** Perhaps the most painful realization was that I felt undervalued, not just by others but by myself. I had spent so much time serving everyone else that I had forgotten to honor my own needs, desires, and dreams. I had lost sight of my own worth.

Each of these states—overwhelmed, underappreciated, overworked, and undervalued—added layers to my disconnection and led me further away from my true self. I began to realize that I was living in a cycle of over-giving and under-receiving, which left me depleted and resentful.

**Recognizing the Symptoms of Burnout and Disconnection**

If you feel like you're in this place of "over-under," take a moment to reflect on these questions:

- Are you constantly exhausted, even after a full night's rest?
- Do you feel a sense of resentment toward the roles and responsibilities in your life?
- Have you lost touch with the things that once brought you joy?
- Do you feel invisible, like your efforts go unrecognized and unappreciated?
- Are you struggling to remember what makes you *you* beyond your roles and obligations?

If you answered "yes" to any of these, you may be experiencing your own version of "The Over-Unders." This is not a weakness; it's a powerful signal that something needs to change. Your soul is craving a reset, a realignment, and a renewal of purpose, power, and passion.

**Embracing the Call for Rebirth**

Recognizing the symptoms of burnout and disconnection isn't just about acknowledging where we are; it's about listening to the call for transformation. For me, "The Over-Unders" were a call to let go of who I had been and step into a new, fuller version of myself. It was time to reconnect with what truly mattered, shed outdated roles and beliefs, and honor the life that was calling me forward.

This stage of my life wasn't just about surviving burnout; it was about stepping into a season of intentional rebirth. Just as the caterpillar must break down completely before transforming into a butterfly, and the eagle must shed its feathers, talons, and beak to emerge anew, I too was in a process of profound shedding and rebuilding. This journey wasn't easy, but it was necessary. It required that I embrace my pain and honor my exhaustion as sacred parts of my journey.

## *The Butterfly's Metamorphosis: Embracing the Beauty in Breakdown*

Transformation, in its truest form, often requires a complete breakdown. A butterfly's journey is one of the most beautiful and profound metaphors for this process. As the caterpillar begins its journey, it lives fully, consuming and growing, moving inch by inch through life. But when it is time for transformation, it does not simply sprout wings and fly. The caterpillar must enter a cocoon—a safe yet confining space where it will experience the ultimate breakdown. Within the cocoon, the caterpillar dissolves into a liquid state, releasing everything it once was, allowing its former self to completely deconstruct.

In this process of dissolution, there is no turning back. The caterpillar lets go of its previous form, fully embracing the unknown, trusting the transformation that lies ahead. This phase of metamorphosis is where the magic happens, but it is not without pain and darkness. The cocoon is dark, isolating, and confining. Inside, the caterpillar is neither what it once was nor what it is yet to become. This in-between state is uncomfortable and vulnerable, yet it is the necessary space for transformation.

As the butterfly finally emerges, it must work its way out of the cocoon, strengthening its wings by pushing against the walls that once held it. The struggle to break free is essential; without it, the butterfly's wings would remain weak, unable to support it in flight. The butterfly's first moments are fragile and tentative, yet its wings gradually gain strength. Eventually, it soars, embodying the beauty of transformation, resilience, and growth.

    Like the butterfly, there are times in our lives when we must allow ourselves to fully break down, to shed all that we have been, and to surrender to the discomfort of transformation. It is a process that requires courage, patience, and faith. The beauty of the butterfly's metamorphosis teaches us that there is purpose in the pain, and that sometimes, we must embrace the breakdown to discover the wings that will carry us forward.

## *The Eagle's Rebirth: Shedding Old Layers to Soar*

The eagle's story of rebirth is a powerful metaphor for shedding old layers to reveal newfound strength. As the eagle reaches middle age, it faces a choice: continue to live with weakened talons, dull feathers, and a beak that no longer serves, or undergo a painful renewal process to soar once more. This decision is not one of mere survival; it is a commitment to reclaiming its power and strength.

When the eagle chooses rebirth, it takes flight to the mountaintop, retreating to a solitary place where it will undergo this demanding process. First, it must break its beak by striking it against a rock. This act is symbolic of releasing old habits, limiting beliefs, and worn-out narratives that no longer serve us. Just as the eagle sheds its beak, we too must be willing to let go of what no longer aligns with who we are becoming.

With a new beak, the eagle then plucks out its talons, allowing stronger ones to grow in their place. This painful act represents the courage it takes to replace outdated ways of thinking and acting with ones that empower us. In life, we often cling to what we know, even when it no longer serves us. But true transformation requires us to let go, trusting that what comes next will be stronger, sharper, and more aligned with our purpose.

Finally, the eagle plucks out its old feathers, allowing fresh, resilient feathers to grow. These new feathers are lighter and stronger, enabling it to soar higher than ever before. For us, this step signifies releasing the identities, roles, or expectations that have weighed us down, making space for a lighter, more authentic self to emerge. This process is not easy; it requires solitude, self-reflection, and an immense amount of trust in the journey.

When the eagle finally takes flight after months of this arduous transformation, it does so with renewed strength, clarity, and purpose. It emerges with wings that can carry it to new heights, talons that can grasp with power, and a beak that symbolizes its ability to communicate its truth.

The eagle's rebirth teaches us that true transformation requires sacrifice and an unyielding commitment to growth. Like the eagle, we must be willing to retreat from the familiar, to release what no longer serves, and to embrace the pain of shedding so that we can soar. This journey is not for the faint of heart, but for those who are ready to reclaim their purpose, power, and passion, it is the path to freedom.

**Reflection: Embracing Your Own Transformation**

Both the butterfly and the eagle show us that transformation is not an easy or instantaneous process. It is a journey that requires breaking down, letting go, and rebuilding. Just as the butterfly must dissolve completely, and the eagle must shed what it has outgrown, we too must be willing to undergo a full reset if we want to reclaim our lives.

Each phase of this journey—whether it's the breakdown of the caterpillar or the shedding of the eagle—holds profound lessons for us. Transformation often requires solitude, patience, and a willingness to embrace discomfort. It demands that we trust the process, even when the outcome is uncertain. By honoring these symbols and their journeys, we are reminded that our own struggles, breakdowns, and moments of release are not signs of weakness, but steps on the path to a more authentic, empowered, and vibrant self.

## Re-negotiate a Contract with Yourself

**Re-Up**: *To re-enlist or re-negotiate a contract.*

In this journey, *Re-Up* is a commitment to yourself—a pledge to stand firmly in your own worth, embrace renewal, and align with your true purpose. It's more than just a decision; it's an active, ongoing choice to re-engage fully with life. Think of it as a sacred agreement to honor yourself, an intentional contract to nurture your dreams and needs as they evolve.

### What It Means to "Re-Up" with Yourself:

1. **Re-Commit**: This is your vow to prioritize your own growth, self-care, and personal well-being. Re-Up means standing in your own corner and committing to a life where you actively nurture yourself first.

2. **Re-Affirm Your Purpose**: Re-Up invites you to revisit and clarify your life's purpose, reconnecting with what brings you joy, fulfillment, and drive. It's about aligning with what matters most and moving forward with renewed focus.

3. **Re-Energize**: This contract includes replenishing your energy, passion, and zest for life. To Re-Up means you are committed to seeking out what fuels you—whether that's rest, connection, or new experiences—to carry you into this next season with vibrancy.

4. **Reclaim Your Power**: Re-Up is also about embracing your unique identity and power. It's a conscious decision to stand in your truth and release any limiting beliefs or roles that no longer serve you.

5. **Revolutionize Your Path**: Finally, Re-Up gives you the freedom to re-envision your journey. It's permission to step outside of your comfort zone and embrace a life aligned with the person you are becoming.

By choosing to *Re-Up*, you are renegotiating the terms of your life with intention. This is your contract—a sacred promise to live in alignment with your highest self, filling your cup first, so you can pour into the world from a place of abundance.

We're going to re-negotiate our contract with ourselves. This is an agreement to:

- Love yourself
- Show yourself grace
- Trust yourself and the process
- Hold space for yourself
- Believe in yourself
- Value yourself
- Honor yourself
- Nurture yourself
- Take care of yourself

- Fill yourself up—first!

This is your moment to commit. This is *the contract.* True transformation requires commitment, so let's make a binding agreement with ourselves to stand in the gap for our own growth.

**Essential Elements of Our Contract**

Each contract requires:

- **Offer** – Set a clear intention.
- **Acceptance** – Embrace this commitment fully.
- **Awareness** – Understand the value of change.
- **Consideration** – Honor your needs and boundaries.
- **Capacity** – Make space for the journey.
- **Legality** – Treat this commitment as sacred.

Find someone to stand with you—a friend or mentor who will hold you accountable, who is willing to support you, encourage you, and go to war with you when needed.

**The 5 Steps to Re-Up**

1. **Step 1: Re-Assess**
   The first step in the re-up is to re-assess. Take inventory of your life. This requires sitting with yourself, embracing stillness, and "cleaning your pallet." It may be uncomfortable, but it's necessary to make room for new blessings. As one of my former leaders at P&G advised, "thin your herd." Clear space in your life for God to move.

2. **Step 2: Re-Imagine**
   Re-imagine who you desire to be—who God has called you to be. Envision your highest potential in vivid detail. What does the heroine of your story look like? How does she walk, talk, dress, and engage? Where does she live? What does she do professionally? Begin to embody her now. Look in the mirror and ask God to reveal to you the woman He has predestined you to become.

3. **Step 3: Re-Invent**
   Re-invent yourself boldly. This step requires a courageous commitment to transformation, including:

   - Protecting your peace at all costs
   - Honoring your word to yourself first
   - Building a village that will support, challenge, and hold you accountable
   - Setting boundaries and using your "No Muscle"
   - Prioritizing radical self-care, ensuring your cup is full

Be intentional, deliberate, and urgent about this process. Move like your life depends on it.

4. **Step 4: Re-Claim**
   Now, it's time to re-claim your purpose, power, and passion. This journey isn't just a phase; it's a new season of life. Tony Robbins speaks about the "seasons of life": Spring is from 0–21, Summer is

from 21–41, and then comes the Power season from 42–63. This season is one of reaping, of reclaiming our leadership, and of stepping fully into our power. I am in the power of my life, and you are too. Now is the time to step forward and claim it.

**Reclaiming Your Purpose, Power, and Passion**

Reclaiming purpose, power, and passion is not a one-time event but a journey. Through the following exercises, you'll reconnect with what truly matters, set strong boundaries, reignite your passions, and find meaning in every step.

1. **Reflect and Realign**
   - Purpose begins with self-awareness. Explore moments that have defined you and dreams that may have been set aside.
   - **Exercise:** Create a "Life Vision Map" that outlines your core values, dreams, and goals. What stands out as your true north?

**Sample Life Vision Map**

1. CORE VALUES

*Identify the guiding principles that shape your life and decisions. These values act as your compass, grounding you in what matters most.*

- **Examples:** Integrity, Compassion, Growth, Courage, Freedom, Family, Faith, Joy, Balance

2. PERSONAL GROWTH & SPIRITUALITY

*Consider how you want to grow personally and spiritually. Reflect on qualities you want to nurture within yourself, or areas where you seek greater fulfillment.*

- **Examples:**
    - Practice daily gratitude and mindfulness.
    - Embrace vulnerability and authenticity.
    - Cultivate inner peace through meditation and prayer.
    - Strengthen your faith or spiritual practice.
    - Commit to continuous learning and self-improvement.

3. RELATIONSHIPS & CONNECTIONS

*Define the kind of relationships you want to build and maintain—with family, friends, mentors, or new connections. Describe the qualities of these relationships and the energy you want to cultivate around you.*

- **Examples:**
    - Build deep, supportive relationships with family and friends.
    - Set healthy boundaries to protect energy and prioritize self-respect.

- Surround yourself with people who uplift, inspire, and challenge you.
- Invest in meaningful heart-to-heart conversations.

### 4. CAREER & PURPOSE

*Envision a career or work life that aligns with your passion and purpose. Consider the impact you want to have and the legacy you want to create.*

- **Examples:**
    - Work that aligns with your values and brings you joy.
    - A role where you can mentor, support, or inspire others.
    - Pursuing leadership roles that allow you to make a meaningful difference.
    - Building a business or brand that uplifts a community or fills a gap.

### 5. HEALTH & WELLNESS

*Describe your vision for physical, mental, and emotional well-being. This includes fitness goals, mental health practices, and habits for self-care.*

- **Examples:**
    - Regular exercise for strength and energy.

- A balanced, nourishing diet.
- Daily practices for mental clarity, like journaling or meditation.
- Adequate rest and relaxation to recharge.
- Embracing self-care practices that nurture your soul.

## 6. FINANCIAL GOALS & ABUNDANCE

*Define your financial vision, including what you want to achieve financially, how you want to feel about money, and how abundance can support your overall vision.*

- **Examples:**
  - Financial independence and freedom from debt.
  - Smart investments that align with your values.
  - Building a legacy fund for family or community.
  - Contributing to causes that matter to you.
  - Practicing gratitude and generosity in your relationship with money.

## 7. LIFESTYLE & ENVIRONMENT

*Imagine the environment and lifestyle that would support your vision. This can include where you live, your ideal daily routines, or activities that bring you joy and fulfillment.*

- **Examples:**
    - Living in a peaceful, nature-centered home.
    - Traveling to broaden your perspective and experience joy.
    - Creating routines that prioritize time for yourself and loved ones.
    - Surrounding yourself with beauty and simplicity.
    - Dedicating time each week to creative or relaxing hobbies.

---

## 8. LEGACY & IMPACT

*Consider the lasting impact you want to make. This may include how you want to be remembered, the difference you want to create, or the contributions you want to make in the lives of others.*

- **Examples:**
    - Empowering others through mentorship or advocacy.
    - Leaving a legacy of kindness, resilience, and compassion.
    - Supporting organizations or causes that align with your values.
    - Making a positive impact in your community.

- Creating a body of work, like a book, that reflects your journey and insights.

**Reflection & Action Steps**

**Reflect on Your Vision**: Look over each area and notice what themes emerge. Are there specific goals, qualities, or intentions that stand out? Consider writing these down as guiding themes or mantras for your journey.

**Create Action Steps**: For each area, set one or two small, actionable steps you can take in the next month to bring you closer to your vision. This may include signing up for a course, scheduling time with loved ones, or adding a new self-care habit.

2. SET BOUNDARIES TO EMPOWER YOURSELF

- Reclaiming power is about protecting your energy.
- **Exercise:** Try "Boundary Building"—identify what drains you and where you need to say "no" to make space for growth.

**Boundary Building Exercise**

Boundaries are essential for protecting our time, energy, and peace. They allow us to honor our needs, set limits on what we're willing to give, and create space for what truly matters. This exercise will help you identify where you need boundaries and guide you in setting them with clarity and confidence.

**Step 1: Reflect on Your Energy Drains**

Begin by identifying situations, relationships, or commitments that feel draining or overwhelming. Ask yourself the following questions:

- What activities or responsibilities leave me feeling exhausted?
- Are there relationships where I often feel taken for granted, unsupported, or resentful?
- Where do I find myself saying "yes" out of obligation, even when I want to say "no"?
- What are the habits or behaviors that prevent me from prioritizing my own well-being?

Take a few minutes to write down your answers. Notice any patterns or areas where you tend to overextend yourself.

**Step 2: Define Your Boundaries**

For each area where you feel drained, consider what boundaries might help protect your energy. Boundaries can be physical, emotional, or time-related, and they should reflect what you need to feel balanced and respected.

- **Examples of Boundaries:**
    - **Time Boundaries**: "I will reserve my mornings for my personal routine and avoid scheduling meetings or tasks before 10 a.m."
    - **Emotional Boundaries**: "I will not engage in conversations that make me feel undervalued or drained."

- **Communication Boundaries**: "I will check my emails only during set hours to avoid feeling overwhelmed."
- **Social Boundaries**: "I will limit time with people who drain my energy, even if it means saying 'no' more often."
- **Work Boundaries**: "I will set limits on how late I work each night to ensure I have time for rest."

**Step 3: Practice Saying "No" with Confidence**

Setting boundaries often means saying "no" to things that don't align with your needs. To get comfortable with this, practice saying "no" in ways that feel respectful but firm. Here are a few phrases you can try:

- "Thank you for thinking of me, but I won't be able to participate this time."
- "I appreciate the invitation, but I need to focus on other priorities right now."
- "That doesn't work for me, but I hope you find the support you need."
- "I'd love to help, but I don't have the capacity right now."

Practice these phrases in front of a mirror or with a friend until you feel comfortable saying "no" without guilt.

**Step 4: Communicate Your Boundaries Clearly**

Once you've defined your boundaries, it's time to communicate them to others as needed. Remember, boundaries are about expressing what you need, not controlling others. When sharing your boundaries, aim for a tone that is calm and clear.

- **Example Boundary Communication**:
    - "I've realized that I need to set some limits to protect my time and energy. I'll be unavailable for meetings before 10 a.m. moving forward to allow myself a productive morning routine. Thanks for understanding."
    - "In order to focus on my own well-being, I'll need to limit our conversations about [specific topic]. I'd love to support you in other ways, but this is something I need to step back from."
    - "I've decided to avoid checking my emails after 7 p.m. so that I can recharge. Please feel free to reach me during the day, and I'll respond promptly then."

**Step 5: Hold Yourself Accountable**

Setting boundaries is just the beginning; maintaining them is key. Holding yourself accountable may involve reminding yourself of why these boundaries matter, noticing when they're being crossed, and gently reinforcing them as needed.

- **Ways to Stay Accountable**:
    - Check in with yourself weekly: Reflect on whether you're honoring your boundaries and if any adjustments are needed.

- Keep a journal: Write about moments when you successfully upheld a boundary and times when it was challenging.
- Celebrate small wins: Acknowledge each time you respect your boundaries as a step toward creating a balanced, intentional life.

3. REDISCOVER JOY AND PLAY
    - Reigniting passion involves rediscovering joy.
    - **Exercise:** Create a "Joy Calendar" where each week you explore a hobby or activity you've loved or always wanted to try.

**Sample Joy Calendar**

**Purpose**: A Joy Calendar encourages us to carve out time for the things that light us up and nurture our spirit. Each week, choose a small activity that makes you feel alive, peaceful, or connected. It doesn't have to be elaborate—sometimes, the simplest acts bring the greatest joy.

**Example One**
**Week 1:**
- **Nature Walk:** Take a peaceful walk in a nearby park or garden. Notice the sounds, sights, and scents around you. Let the beauty of nature bring you calm and grounding.

- **Morning Dance Party (Mid-Week):** Start your day with your favorite song and let yourself dance freely for a few minutes. Move however you feel and let joy flow through your body.

- **At-Home Spa Day (Weekend):** Set aside time for a self-care ritual, like a bath with essential oils, a face mask, or simply relaxing with a warm cup of tea. Create a peaceful space and pamper yourself.

**Week 2:**

- **Gratitude Journal:** Each morning or evening, write down three things you're grateful for. This simple practice helps cultivate a sense of joy and appreciation.

- **Creative Play (Mid-Week):** Spend 30 minutes drawing, painting, or doing any creative activity that brings you joy. Don't worry about perfection—just have fun!

- **Coffee or Tea Date (Weekend):** Visit a local cafe or create a special coffee or tea ritual at home. Savor each sip and let this moment be all about relaxation.

**Week 3:**

- **Meditation or Quiet Reflection:** Set aside 10 minutes each day for quiet reflection or meditation. Sit in a comfortable spot, focus on your breath, and let this moment be for you alone.

- **Reconnect with an Old Friend (Mid-Week):** Schedule a call or FaceTime with someone who uplifts you. Share laughter, memories, and connect heart-to-heart.

- **Explore a New Book or Podcast (Weekend):** Find a book or podcast that inspires or entertains you. Take time to dive into new ideas and let yourself be immersed in a fresh perspective.

**Week 4:**

- **Declutter and Create Space:** Choose one small area to declutter—a desk, a drawer, or a corner of a room. Clearing physical space often brings mental clarity and a feeling of lightness.

- **Try a New Recipe or Dish (Mid-Week):** Cook or try a new recipe, or treat yourself to a dish you love. Enjoy the process and savor each bite as a celebration of flavor and nourishment.

- **Sunrise or Sunset Moment (Weekend):** Set aside time to watch a sunrise or sunset. Let this natural beauty remind you of the simple wonders around you.

---

**Tips for Creating Your Own Joy Calendar**

- **Mix It Up**: Include a variety of activities, from creative play and self-care to connection and reflection.

- **Keep It Simple**: Joyful moments don't have to be time-consuming or costly. The aim is to create intentional moments that nourish your spirit.
- **Adjust as Needed**: Each month, try different activities or repeat the ones you enjoy most. Customize the calendar to reflect what brings *you* the most joy.
- **Reflect on Your Joy**: At the end of each week, take a moment to reflect on how each activity made you feel. Over time, you'll gain insight into what truly uplifts and energizes you.

4. PRACTICE DAILY GRATITUDE AND AFFIRMATIONS
    - Purpose, power, and passion are nurtured by gratitude.
    - **Exercise:** Keep a "Gratitude & Affirmation Journal" to affirm your progress and celebrate your journey.

**Gratitude & Affirmation Journal Prompts**

**Purpose**: Gratitude and affirmation journaling helps cultivate a positive mindset, enhances self-awareness, and reinforces personal growth. These prompts are designed to guide you in focusing on the good in your life and in affirming your worth and potential.

## Gratitude Prompts

1. **Morning Gratitude**: *What is one thing I'm looking forward to today? How can I approach it with a grateful heart?*

2. **Celebrating Small Wins**: *What's one small accomplishment or step forward I made today? Why am I proud of this?*

3. **Relationships**: *Who in my life am I most grateful for today, and why? How has this person made a positive impact on me?*

4. **Gratitude for Challenges**: *What recent challenge has taught me something valuable? How has it helped me grow or see things in a new light?*

5. **Gratitude in Nature**: *What natural beauty did I notice today (a tree, the sky, a sunset) that made me pause and appreciate the moment?*

6. **Self-Gratitude**: *What is one quality or strength of mine that I'm grateful for? How has it helped me overcome obstacles or feel more empowered?*

7. **Past Gratitude**: *Think of a difficult experience from the past that you can now appreciate for the lessons it taught you. How did it shape who you are today?*

8. **Daily Gratitude Reflection**: *What are three things, big or small, that I am grateful for today?*

**Affirmation Prompts**

1. **Morning Affirmation**: *What affirmation do I want to carry with me throughout today? How can it support me in feeling confident and grounded?*
2. **Self-Love Affirmation**: *What positive words do I need to hear today? Write an affirmation that reminds me of my worth and strength.*
3. **Overcoming Challenges**: *What is a challenge I am facing right now? Write an affirmation that empowers me to move through it with resilience and courage.*
4. **Personal Strengths**: *What are three qualities I admire in myself? Create affirmations around each one to reinforce their importance in my life.*
5. **Future Vision**: *Imagine your future self living a life of fulfillment and purpose. What affirmation can I create that connects me to this vision?*
6. **Affirming Change**: *What is one change I'm working toward? Write an affirmation that supports this transformation and encourages me to keep going.*
7. **Peace and Balance**: *What affirmation would bring me peace right now? How can I remind myself to slow down and trust the process?*
8. **Reflection and Growth**: *What affirmation speaks to my journey of growth? How can I affirm my commitment to becoming the best version of myself?*

**Sample Journal Entry**

Consider starting your day by selecting one gratitude prompt and one affirmation prompt, then write your responses in a journal. For example:

---

**Date: [Insert Date]**

**Gratitude Prompt:** *What are three things, big or small, that I am grateful for today?*

- I'm grateful for the sunshine this morning, which lifted my spirits and gave me energy.
- I'm thankful for a conversation I had with a friend who really listened and supported me.
- I appreciate the quiet moments in my day that give me space to reflect and breathe.

**Affirmation Prompt:** *What positive words do I need to hear today?*

- *I am worthy of love and respect, and I choose to honor my own needs and boundaries.*

5. VISUALIZE AND TAKE ACTION
    - Visualize the life you desire, then take small steps to realize it.
    - **Exercise:** Make a vision board and take one action each day that moves you closer to your dreams.

**Sample Vision Board Template**

**Center: Core Intention or Theme**

*Place a word, phrase, or image in the center that represents your overall intention or theme for this vision board. This could be a word like "Growth," "Joy," "Balance," or a short phrase like "Embracing My Purpose."*

**Top Left Corner: Personal Growth & Wellness**

- **Images**: Choose images that reflect your ideal physical, mental, and emotional well-being.

- **Words/Quotes**: Add words like "Health," "Energy," "Calm," or quotes that inspire your wellness journey.

- **Examples**: A picture of a sunrise for a morning routine, healthy foods, a yoga pose, or an affirmation about self-care.

**Top Right Corner: Relationships & Connection**

- **Images**: Add photos or images that represent family, friendships, community, and love.

- **Words/Quotes**: Words like "Love," "Support," "Connection," or phrases about meaningful relationships.

- **Examples**: A heart symbol, images of people holding hands, or a quote like, "Surround yourself with those who lift you higher."

### Bottom Left Corner: Career & Purpose

- **Images**: Add visuals that represent your professional goals, passions, and purpose-driven work.

- **Words/Quotes**: Phrases like "Impact," "Success," "Creativity," or quotes that inspire your work.

- **Examples**: A picture of a stage for public speaking, a pen for writing, or a powerful quote about making a difference.

### Bottom Right Corner: Lifestyle & Abundance

- **Images**: Represent your ideal lifestyle, financial goals, and personal abundance.

- **Words/Quotes**: Words like "Freedom," "Abundance," "Adventure," or quotes about living fully.

- **Examples**: Photos of places you want to travel, symbols of financial freedom, or a quote like, "Live with purpose, abundance, and joy."

### Additional Sections or Visuals (Optional)

- **Spirituality**: Include symbols or quotes related to your spiritual beliefs or practices.

- **Hobbies & Passions**: Represent interests you want to explore, like art, music, or sports.

- **Affirmations**: Include a few personal affirmations that resonate with your vision.

**Tips for Creating Your Vision Board**

1. **Collect Materials**: Use magazines, printouts, or digital images for your board. Choose items that truly resonate with you and your goals.

2. **Personalize It**: Arrange images, words, and quotes in a way that feels natural. You can use a corkboard, poster board, or a digital format.

3. **Display It Proudly**: Place your vision board somewhere you'll see it daily to remind yourself of your intentions and keep you motivated.

6. BUILD YOUR POWER CIRCLE

    - Surround yourself with people who inspire, challenge, and uplift you.

    - **Exercise:** Connect with those who energize you and seek new connections that share your values.

**Building Your Power Circle: Template**

**Purpose:** Use this template to list individuals in your life who bring out the best in you. These are the people who energize, inspire, challenge, and uplift you. Having a Power Circle helps you stay grounded, motivated, and supported in your journey.

**Power Circle**

1. **[Name _____]**

    ***Role in My Life*:** Mentor, friend, or colleague.

    ***Qualities They Bring*:** Wise, encouraging, and experienced.

    ***How They Uplift Me*:** Provides guidance and encourages me to reach my goals.

2. **[Name _____]**

    ***Role in My Life*:** Family member, peer, or coach.

    ***Qualities They Bring*:** Positive, resilient, and honest.

    ***How They Uplift Me*:** Listens without judgment and motivates me to be my best.

3. **[Name _____]**

    ***Role in My Life*:** Supportive friend or partner.

    ***Qualities They Bring*:** Compassionate, inspiring, and creative.

    ***How They Uplift Me*:** Inspires my creativity and offers new perspectives.

4. **[Name _____]**

   ***Role in My Life***: Accountability partner or peer.

   ***Qualities They Bring***: Challenging, reliable, and empathetic.

   ***How They Uplift Me***: Holds me accountable and helps me stay focused.

5. **[Name _____]**

   ***Role in My Life***: Spiritual advisor or teacher.

   ***Qualities They Bring***: Insightful, grounded, and supportive.

   ***How They Uplift Me***: Brings me clarity and supports my spiritual growth.

6. **[Name _____]**

   ***Role in My Life***: Professional network contact.

   ***Qualities They Bring***: Resourceful, connected, and knowledgeable.

   ***How They Uplift Me***: Provides industry insights and opens doors for opportunities.

**Reflection Questions**

- **Who Energizes You?**
  *Who are the people that leave you feeling uplifted and energized after spending time with them?*

- **Who Inspires You?**
  *Who in your life embodies qualities or values that you admire? Who do you look up to as a role model?*

- **Who Challenges You?**
  *Who encourages you to step out of your comfort zone, think critically, or take positive risks?*

- **Who Uplifts You?**
  *Who offers support, listens without judgment, and cheers you on through highs and lows?*

**Using Your Power Circle**

- **Connect Regularly**: Make a commitment to reach out to each person in your Power Circle regularly. Schedule a coffee date, video call, or a simple check-in.

- **Express Gratitude**: Show appreciation for their presence in your life and the ways they've contributed to your growth.

- **Reciprocate**: A Power Circle is reciprocal. Offer support, encouragement, and motivation to these individuals, creating a mutually uplifting relationship.

7. **CELEBRATE YOUR PROGRESS**
    - Recognize each small victory as a step forward.
    - **Exercise:** Keep a "Win Log" to record achievements and reflect on your growth.

**Win Log Template**

**Purpose:** Use this log to record daily or weekly wins, no matter how small. Reflecting on your accomplishments helps you recognize progress, build momentum, and stay connected to your growth. Wins can be anything that made you feel proud, happy, or aligned with your goals.

**Sample Win Log**

- **Date**: [MM/DD/YYYY]
  **Win or Achievement**: Completed my morning workout
  **Why This Matters**: Staying committed to my health goals and building discipline
  **Feelings/Reflection**: Felt strong and proud of sticking to my plan

- **Date**: [MM/DD/YYYY]
  **Win or Achievement**: Said "no" to a commitment
  **Why This Matters**: Protected my time and set a boundary for self-care
  **Feelings/Reflection**: Felt empowered and more in control of my schedule

- **Date**: [MM/DD/YYYY]
  **Win or Achievement**: Reached out to a mentor for advice

**Why This Matters**: Taking action on professional growth and building connections
**Feelings/Reflection**: Appreciated their insights and felt more motivated

- **Date**: [MM/DD/YYYY]
  **Win or Achievement**: Spent quality time with family
  **Why This Matters**: Nurturing relationships that matter to me
  **Feelings/Reflection**: Felt connected, loved, and supported

- **Date**: [MM/DD/YYYY]
  **Win or Achievement**: Took 10 minutes for meditation
  **Why This Matters**: Focusing on mental clarity and self-care
  **Feelings/Reflection**: Felt peaceful and centered afterward

**Reflection Prompts**

At the end of each week, use these prompts to reflect on your wins and progress:

1. **What did I learn from my wins this week?**
2. **How did these achievements make me feel about my goals and journey?**
3. **Is there a specific area where I'd like to focus more next week?**

4. How can I build on these successes moving forward?

**Tips for Using Your Win Log**

- **Record Small Wins**: Remember, a win doesn't have to be monumental. Even small victories, like staying positive in a challenging situation, are worth celebrating.

- **Consistency**: Try to fill in your log daily or weekly to maintain momentum and keep a record of your progress over time.

- **Celebrate Yourself**: At the end of each week or month, review your log and acknowledge how far you've come. Recognize the effort and growth you're putting into your journey.

Each exercise is an invitation to live with intention. Embrace this journey as a commitment to yourself—a journey that reconnects you with the purpose, power, and passion that has always been within you.

## Filling Your Cup: The Art of Soul Care

As we navigate life's many demands, it's easy to forget the importance of caring for ourselves. We give so much to others—our time, energy, and love—that we often leave ourselves running on empty. But true transformation requires a full cup. Soul care isn't a luxury; it's a necessity. It's about honoring ourselves and replenishing our spirit so that we can show up fully in all areas of life.

In this section, we'll explore ways to fill your cup with practices that nurture and restore. I'll share some of my own go-to soul care rituals, from affirmations and music that uplift me to simple moments of joy and peace that bring me back to center. I invite you to discover what fills you up, to create your own affirmations, and to reconnect with yourself through the healing power of music and intentional self-care.

This is a space for you to embrace what feels good to your soul. Here, we're not just pouring into ourselves; we're creating a wellspring of love, joy, and peace that can overflow into everything we do. So take a breath, set aside any guilt, and let's explore the art of filling your cup.

## **Affirmations for the Journey**

Affirmations are powerful statements that help us shift our mindset and ground ourselves in positivity. They serve as reminders of our worth, resilience, and purpose. Creating affirmations is a deeply personal exercise; the key is to craft words that truly resonate with you. Here is a set of affirmations to inspire you. Feel free to use these, adapt them, or create your own.

### **Sample Affirmations:**

- I am worthy of love, peace, and abundance.
- I am whole and complete, just as I am.
- I trust the process of transformation and embrace the journey.
- My past does not define me; I am free to create the life I desire.

- I fill my cup with kindness, compassion, and joy.
- I honor my needs and respect my boundaries.
- I am open to new possibilities and align with my highest self.
- I have the strength and courage to live fully and authentically.

**Exercise: Crafting Your Personal Affirmations**

1. **Reflect on Your Journey**: Think about where you are right now and where you'd like to go. What qualities do you want to nurture in yourself? What words do you need to hear?

2. **Write Down Your Affirmations**: Start with a phrase like "I am," "I choose," or "I embrace." Make it positive, specific, and in the present tense, as if it is already true.

3. **Speak It Daily**: Place your affirmations where you'll see them regularly—on your mirror, phone screen, or journal. Repeat them aloud each morning, letting their energy fill your spirit.

## Healing Through Music: Creating a Soulful Playlist

Music has the power to heal, uplift, and connect us to our emotions. For me, music is like medicine for the soul. It can be a source of strength, joy, and release. Curating a playlist of songs that feel good to your soul is a powerful form of self-care, a way to hold space for yourself and uplift your spirit.

**Exercise: Create Your Soul Playlist**

1. **Set Your Intention**: Think about what you want this playlist to bring into your life. Is it peace, empowerment, joy, or healing? Set an intention to create a playlist that aligns with that.

2. **Select Your Songs**: Choose songs that resonate deeply with you—songs that make you feel alive, bring comfort, or transport you to a positive place. Include any genre, decade, or artist that speaks to you.

3. **Name Your Playlist**: Give your playlist a title that reflects its purpose, like "Soul Healing," "Feel-Good Vibes," or "Peaceful Moments." Let this be your go-to playlist whenever you need a boost.

4. **Listen Intentionally**: Whenever you need a moment of reprieve or connection, put on your playlist. Allow the music to guide you, feeling the beat, lyrics, and rhythm as they flow through you.

**Soul Care Practices: Filling Your Cup**

Soul care is essential to feeling balanced, whole, and at peace. It's about nurturing yourself with practices that bring joy, comfort, and grounding. Here are some soul care practices to help you fill your cup. These are ideas I personally love, and you may find they resonate with you or inspire new practices of your own.

**Ideas to Fill Your Cup**

1. **Dance Freely**: Put on a song you love, close the door, and just dance. Let go of any judgment and move in whatever way feels natural. Dancing is a beautiful release that allows you to reconnect with your body and spirit.

2. **Sit in Silence**: Wrap yourself in a soft blanket and just be. Let yourself sit in silence, taking deep breaths and allowing your thoughts to quiet. This simple practice brings calm and helps you reconnect with yourself.

3. **Tea and a Good Book**: Brew a cup of hot tea, settle into a cozy spot, and dive into an audiobook or physical book that feeds your mind and soul. The combination of warmth, words, and stillness can feel incredibly nurturing.

4. **Take a Nature Walk**: Step outside and walk in a nearby park or garden. Feel the ground beneath your feet, listen to the sounds around you, and breathe in the fresh air. Nature has a gentle way of grounding us and restoring peace.

5. **Heart-to-Heart Connections**: Schedule a FaceTime with a sister friend for a deep, soulful conversation. Sharing your heart and listening to someone else's can fill you up in ways that few things can. These connections remind us of our shared journey and our resilience.

**Exercise: Discovering Your Own Soul Care Practices**

1. **Reflect on What Fills You Up**: Think about times when you've felt deeply at peace, joyful, or content. What activities brought you that feeling? Make a list of those moments.

2. **Try Something New**: Explore new soul care practices if you're unsure where to start. Try journaling, painting, taking a long bath, or meditating. Allow yourself to experiment without judgment.

3. **Make It a Ritual**: Choose one or two practices that resonate with you and make them part of your weekly or daily routine. Treat this time as sacred, knowing that by filling your cup, you're able to give more fully to yourself and others.

**Step 5: Re-Emerge – Embracing Your New Self**

Re-emergence is the moment when all the inner work, the breaking down, and the rebuilding come together. It's the phase where you step forward, embodying the person you have become, with the strength, wisdom, and self-love gained through your journey. To re-emerge is to rise fully into the most authentic, empowered version of yourself, unburdened by past limitations.

In the process of transformation, the re-emergence stage is akin to a butterfly unfurling its wings or an eagle taking flight after months of renewal. You've shed old patterns, redefined your values, and filled your cup, and now it's time to soar. Re-emergence isn't about being perfect; it's about being whole, confident, and connected to who you truly are. Here's how to embrace this new chapter and carry it forward.

### 1. Own Your Story and Your Strength

You've gone through a powerful journey that required courage, patience, and resilience. Owning your story is the foundation of re-emergence. It means recognizing the strength you gained from challenges and acknowledging that each step of your journey has shaped you.

- Affirmation: *"I honor my journey, and I am proud of the strength it has given me."*
- Action Step: Take time to journal about the growth you've experienced. Reflect on the moments of courage, the lessons learned, and how these have contributed to your new sense of self.

### 2. Step into Your Vision with Confidence

Re-emergence calls you to step into the vision you've created for your life. This isn't just about visualizing who you want to be—it's about living as that person every day. You have clarified your values, set intentions, and envisioned a life of purpose, power, and passion. Now, it's time to embody that vision fully.

- Affirmation: *"I am living my vision with confidence and purpose."*
- Action Step: Identify one or two actions that align with your vision. This could be starting a new morning ritual, setting healthy boundaries, or pursuing a goal with renewed commitment. Treat

these actions as a reflection of your new, empowered self.

### 3. Embrace Self-Compassion and Flexibility

Re-emergence is not about maintaining a rigid ideal; it's about nurturing yourself and allowing space to evolve. Life will continue to bring challenges, but you now have the tools to handle them with grace. Embrace self-compassion as a core part of your re-emergence, recognizing that growth is ongoing and that setbacks are simply opportunities to learn.

- Affirmation: *"I allow myself to grow at my own pace, with love and compassion."*
- Action Step: When facing challenges, practice self-compassion by speaking to yourself as you would to a close friend. Remind yourself that you are allowed to be both a work in progress and a masterpiece.

### 4. Live Aligned with Your Values

In this new chapter, commit to making choices that reflect your core values and true desires. Living in alignment with your values means saying "yes" to what fills you with purpose and "no" to what drains you. By doing this, you're honoring your journey and the transformation you've achieved.

- Affirmation: *"I make choices that honor my values and uplift my spirit."*
- Action Step: Write down your top three values. For each value, consider one way you can honor it in your daily life. For example, if "Health" is a core

value, commit to a nourishing morning routine that supports your well-being.

### 5. Surround Yourself with Your Power Circle

You are the sum of the people who uplift, inspire, and encourage you. Re-emerging into a new chapter is not something you do alone; it's supported by those who believe in your growth and who reflect the energy you want in your life. Lean on your Power Circle to keep you grounded and motivated.

- Affirmation: *"I am surrounded by people who support, uplift, and encourage my growth."*
- Action Step: Make a list of people who bring positive energy into your life. Schedule regular check-ins or gatherings with these individuals to maintain a supportive community around you.

### 6. Celebrate Your Re-Emergence

Finally, honor this stage by celebrating your journey and the new self you've become. Recognize that re-emergence is both an arrival and a new beginning. Mark this moment with something meaningful—a small ritual, a quiet reflection, or a joyful gathering with loved ones.

- Affirmation: *"I celebrate my growth, and I am ready to embrace the journey ahead with joy and gratitude."*
- Action Step: Create a "Re-Emergence Ritual" to honor your transformation. This could be lighting a candle as a symbol of your new chapter, taking a

solo trip to reflect, or hosting a small gathering with friends to celebrate your growth.

## Re-Emerge: Embrace Your Highest Self with Confidence and Grace

Re-emergence is not a destination; it's a continuous commitment to live as the empowered person you are becoming. With each day, you'll strengthen your connection to your purpose, power, and passion. As you re-emerge, remind yourself that you are worthy of every good thing that comes into your life. You have done the work, embraced the journey, and now you're ready to soar.

Affirmation for Re-Emergence
*"I am resilient, I am powerful, and I am fully embracing this new chapter of my life with purpose, joy, and gratitude."*

Reflection Questions:

1. What does re-emergence mean to me personally? How do I envision my life moving forward?

2. What are three qualities I want to embody in this new chapter?

3. How will I honor my growth and continue nurturing my transformation?

## Embracing Your Village of Support: The Power of Community in Re-Emergence

As you step forward in your re-emergence, one essential element will amplify and sustain your growth: your village. This village is your circle of support, the people who love, uplift, and stand by you. It includes your spouse or partner, your children, your family, and close friends. These individuals are not just witnesses to your journey—they are a vital part of it.

Re-emergence is a deeply personal journey, but it's also one that is supported and strengthened by the connections around you. Having a healthy and strong village of support reminds you that you're never alone, no matter where life leads. This village celebrates your wins, helps you stay grounded, and offers love and encouragement during challenges. Let's explore the impact of a strong village of support and how to nurture these connections.

**1. The Role of Loved Ones in Your Journey**

Your loved ones—whether it's a spouse, partner, children, or family—provide a foundation of unconditional support. They see you at your best and your worst and continue to offer love, compassion, and acceptance. Their presence keeps you anchored, reminding you of the person you are beyond titles, roles, or achievements. After re-emergence, the strength and understanding of these core relationships help you thrive in your new chapter.

- **Spouse/Partner**: Your partner is often a primary source of support, someone who believes in your potential and stands by you. Their encouragement empowers you to pursue your goals confidently, knowing they're cheering you on.

- **Children**: Your children learn from your journey, watching as you model resilience, self-love, and purpose. They are your legacy, inspired by your courage to embrace growth.

- **Family**: Family members share your history and know the depths of your journey. Their support helps ground you in your roots while you move forward with strength.

## 2. Friends and Chosen Family: Companions on the Journey

Friends are the companions you choose, people who understand your dreams and share in your highs and lows. These are the people who check in, offer a listening ear, and celebrate every step of your progress. Friends in your village remind you to laugh, stay present, and enjoy the journey, bringing an element of joy and lightness that only true friends can.

- **Celebrating Wins Together**: Friends are often the first to celebrate your victories, big or small. They see your progress and validate the work you've put in, helping you appreciate how far you've come.

- **Offering Honest Support**: True friends challenge you when needed and encourage you to stay aligned with your goals. They offer the kind of honesty that's rooted in care, guiding you back to your path when you waver.

- **Creating Joyful Memories**: Friendship is a wellspring of joy and shared experiences. These moments of laughter, celebration, and connection refill your cup, ensuring that you are both grounded and fulfilled.

### 3. Community and Mentors: Expanding Your Circle of Influence

While family and close friends form the heart of your village, your broader community and mentors also play a vital role. Mentors provide guidance and perspective, helping you grow in ways that family and friends may not. Your community, whether it's professional, spiritual, or personal, offers connection and belonging that supports your journey.

- **Mentors**: A mentor's wisdom can be transformative, helping you see opportunities, overcome challenges, and grow into your fullest potential. They are often people who have walked a similar path and can offer insight and encouragement.

- **Community Networks**: Surrounding yourself with like-minded people who share your values and passions reinforces your growth. Whether it's a support group, a spiritual community, or a professional network, these groups give you a sense of purpose and connection beyond yourself.

### 4. Building and Maintaining a Healthy Village

Having a supportive village is crucial, but maintaining it requires intention and care. Like any relationship, these connections thrive when they are nurtured with time, honesty, and gratitude. Here are some ways to cultivate a healthy and strong village:

- **Express Gratitude**: Regularly show appreciation to the people in your village. Let them know the impact they have on your life and thank them for their presence and support.

- **Communicate Openly**: Share your goals, struggles, and growth with your village. Open, honest communication strengthens bonds and helps others understand and support your journey.
- **Reciprocate Support**: A healthy village is reciprocal. Be present for your loved ones, celebrate their wins, and offer support during their challenges. Investing in these relationships deepens the connection and mutual trust.
- **Schedule Quality Time**: Make time to connect regularly with the people in your village. These moments, whether a simple coffee date, a phone call, or family dinner, are essential for keeping relationships strong and meaningful.

**5. The Impact of a Strong Village on Your Re-Emergence**

After re-emergence, your village serves as both a mirror and a refuge. They reflect back to you the strength and growth you may not always see, reinforcing your confidence and sense of purpose. They provide a safe place to lean on during tough times and a joyful space to celebrate during victories. A strong village ensures that, as you move forward, you do so with a foundation of love, support, and shared joy.

- **Grounding You in Truth**: Your village reminds you of who you are when life gets challenging.

They offer perspective, keeping you grounded and focused on what truly matters.

- **Encouraging You to Grow**: Growth doesn't stop with re-emergence; it's a lifelong journey. Your village continues to encourage you to pursue your dreams, embrace new opportunities, and live authentically.

- **Celebrating Life Together**: Shared experiences and celebrations create lasting memories. The joy of celebrating life's moments with your village adds depth and richness to your journey.

**Reflection: Embracing Your Village with Gratitude**

As you continue forward, remember to cherish the people who stand with you. Take time to reflect on the impact they have on your life and honor them as part of your journey. Embracing a village of support isn't just about receiving—it's about sharing, giving back, and celebrating the journey together. Your re-emergence is amplified by the love, encouragement, and resilience of those around you.

**Affirmation**: *"I am surrounded by a village of love, support, and encouragement. Together, we uplift and empower each other to live fully and joyfully."*

**Action Step**: Choose one way to celebrate your village this week. Write a thank-you note, host a gathering, or simply reach out to let them know how much they mean to you. Embrace the joy of community and let it fuel your continued journey.

In this way, your village becomes not just a source of support, but a powerful foundation upon which you can continue to build, grow, and thrive. Together, you create a life of connection, resilience, and shared purpose.

## **The Village Gathering: A Celebration of Rebirth and Re-Emergence**

After re-emerging into a new chapter of life, there is immense power in sharing your journey with those who have supported you along the way. A **Village Gathering** is a personal, symbolic gathering where you bring together your closest family, friends, and supporters to share your story of tests, triumphs, and transformation. This isn't just a celebration; it's a deeply spiritual and healing experience that honors the growth you've achieved and the love that surrounds you.

The Village Gathering can be as intimate or as expansive as you wish. It's about creating a space that feels true to you—a moment to honor your rebirth and invite your loved ones to celebrate your journey with you. Here's how to make this gathering a powerful experience that marks your re-emergence in a meaningful and lasting way.

### **1. Setting the Intention for Your Village Gathering**

The purpose of a Village Gathering is to create a sacred space where you can reflect on your journey, express gratitude to your support circle, and celebrate your progress. Begin by setting an intention for the gathering. This intention can be as simple as giving thanks for the love and support you've received or as profound as celebrating a new season of purpose, strength, and joy.

- **Sample Intentions**:
    - *"To honor the strength within me and the love of those who supported me."*
    - *"To give thanks for the lessons learned and celebrate the path ahead with my loved ones."*
    - *"To mark this moment of transformation and share my story of resilience and re-emergence."*

Setting an intention helps ground the gathering, making it a purposeful and healing experience for everyone involved.

## 2. Creating a Healing and Joyful Atmosphere

A Village Gathering is both a celebration and a spiritual experience, so creating the right atmosphere is essential. Consider elements that bring a sense of peace, joy, and unity to the space.

- **Food**: Prepare or share a meal that feels nourishing and celebratory. Food is a powerful symbol of love and connection, and sharing a meal can create an atmosphere of warmth and intimacy. Whether it's a home-cooked meal, a catered gathering, or a potluck where everyone brings something meaningful, let the food be a reflection of the gratitude and love that fills the gathering.
- **Healing Music**: Music holds a unique ability to heal, uplift, and connect people. Choose songs that resonate with your journey or bring peace and joy to

the space. Healing music could include soft instrumental tunes, worship songs, soulful melodies, or tracks that have been a source of strength for you. Consider creating a playlist that you can share with your guests afterward as a reminder of the gathering.

- **Personal Touches**: Add symbols or elements that hold meaning for you. This could include candles, flowers, quotes that inspired you, or photos that capture your journey. Each of these touches adds depth to the experience, making it a true reflection of your rebirth and resilience.

### 3. Sharing Your Story of Tests and Triumphs

One of the most powerful aspects of the Village Gathering is the moment when you share your story with those who have been part of your journey. This can be a heartfelt reflection on the challenges you've overcome, the lessons you've learned, and the ways you've grown. It's a testimony to your strength and an opportunity to give thanks for the people who stood by you.

- **Reflect on Your Journey**: Consider the highs and lows, the pivotal moments that shaped you, and the resilience that brought you here. Speak from the heart, and let your loved ones know the impact they've had on your journey.

- **Express Gratitude**: Acknowledge each person in your village and the specific ways they've supported, encouraged, or uplifted you. Expressing gratitude not only honors them but also deepens your connection and solidifies the bonds that helped you through.

- **Invite Reflection**: Allow space for others to share their reflections, words of encouragement, or even their own journeys. A Village Gathering is a shared experience, and inviting your loved ones to participate creates a sense of unity and collective healing.

### 4. Making It Symbolic and Spiritual

The Village Gathering is more than a gathering; it's a rite of passage and a deeply spiritual moment. Incorporate symbolic acts or rituals that mark your re-emergence and invite healing energy into the space.

- **Lighting a Candle or Symbolic Object**: Begin the gathering by lighting a candle, sage, or any item that holds spiritual significance to you. This can represent letting go of the past and welcoming the light of a new beginning. Invite your guests to reflect on the meaning of this moment as you transition into a new chapter.

- **Affirmations or Blessings**: End the gathering with affirmations or blessings that honor the journey of everyone involved. You could write an affirmation for each person or create a collective affirmation for the group. A blessing, prayer, or moment of silence can also be a powerful way to close the gathering and express gratitude for the support you've received.

**5. Making the Village Gathering a Tradition**

For many, transformation is an ongoing journey, and the Village Gathering can become a tradition that you return to as you continue to grow. Consider hosting a Village Gathering annually or after each significant milestone. This gathering not only celebrates your journey but strengthens the bonds within your support circle, reminding everyone of the power of love, resilience, and community.

**Reflection: The Power of a Village Gathering**

A Village Gathering is a testament to the love and resilience that fuel transformation. It's an opportunity to celebrate, heal, and connect with those who have walked beside you. By sharing your story, honoring your support circle, and creating a space for collective reflection, you are both embracing your re-emergence and inviting your loved ones to share in the beauty of your journey.

**Affirmation**: *"I honor my journey and celebrate the strength of my village. Together, we lift each other up, heal, and move forward in love."*

**Action Step**: If you feel called, plan your own Village Gathering. Choose a setting, invite your village, and prepare to share your story. Let this gathering be a powerful and healing moment that marks your re-emergence and celebrates the love that surrounds you.

A Village Gathering is a beautiful way to honor your re-emergence, deepen your connections, and celebrate the transformative power of community. Through food, music, storytelling, and shared reflection, you are creating a sacred space for healing, love, and joy. This gathering becomes a symbol of your resilience and a reminder that you are never alone on your journey.

---

With each step, you are redefining and reclaiming yourself. You're not just "re-upping" for life—you're preparing for your most powerful season yet.

---

## The Contract

**Personal Contract for Transformation and Soul Care**

*This is a commitment to myself—a sacred contract to honor, nurture, and empower my journey toward wholeness and authenticity. By signing this contract, I agree to pour into my life with the same dedication I give to others, holding space for my growth and well-being.*

---

**Section 1: My Commitment**

I, _____, commit to:

1. **Honor my needs** by actively listening to what my body, mind, and spirit require.

2. **Practice self-compassion** and show myself the grace to grow without judgment.

3. **Set and uphold boundaries** that protect my energy and peace.

4. **Pursue joy, passion, and purpose** by aligning my actions with my heart's true desires.

5. **Allow rest and rejuvenation**, knowing that taking time for myself is essential to my well-being.

6. **Fill my cup** by engaging in practices that nourish my soul.

## Section 2: Affirmations of Intention

*Each time I read this contract, I will affirm the following truths about myself and my journey:*

- I am worthy of love, peace, and joy.
- I choose to prioritize my well-being.
- I give myself permission to grow, change, and release what no longer serves me.
- I am committed to living fully, with purpose and intention.
- I honor my unique journey and trust the process of transformation.

---

## Section 3: My Soul Care Practices

*To honor this contract, I will intentionally engage in practices that fill my cup. My chosen soul care practices include:*

1. **[e.g., Daily affirmations that uplift and empower me]**

   _____

   _____

2. **[e.g., Curating a playlist of songs that heal my spirit and make me feel alive]**

   _____

   _____

3. [e.g., Taking a walk in nature each week to reconnect with peace and clarity]

_____

_____

4. [e.g., Setting aside time for silence and reflection in a comforting space]

_____

_____

5. [e.g., Having heart-to-heart conversations with a close friend for mutual support]

_____

_____

*(Fill in each line with personal soul care practices that resonate with you.)*

**Section 4: Accountability Partner**

**Name of Accountability Partner:** _____

*Transformation is a journey best shared. I choose to invite [Accountability Partner's Name] into this process, trusting them to support, encourage, and hold me accountable. I commit to sharing my challenges and successes with them as I navigate this journey.*

### Section 5: My Signature of Commitment

By signing this contract, I am declaring my dedication to myself, to my growth, and to my healing. I will revisit this contract regularly to remind myself of my worth, my commitment, and the beauty of transformation.

Signature: _____

Date: _____

### Reflection & Renewal

*Each month, I will return to this contract to reflect on my progress, celebrate my growth, and renew my commitment to myself. I may adjust my soul care practices as I evolve, ensuring that they continue to fill my cup and support my journey.*

## A Heartfelt Thank You

Dear reader,

Thank you for trusting yourself enough to embark on this journey and for allowing me to walk alongside you. Writing this book has been a labor of love, and knowing it might serve as a light for your path fills my heart with gratitude. You have chosen a path of transformation, one that takes courage and intention, and that alone is worth celebrating. Every step you've taken and each moment of self-reflection speaks to the love you have for yourself.

This journey, the Re-Up, isn't a one-time experience. It's a process we return to, gaining deeper insight and renewed strength each time. Life has a way of leading us back to these moments when we need them most. Embrace this journey at your own pace, honoring the beautiful, resilient person you are becoming. Remember, you can reassess, reimagine, and reemerge as often as your spirit needs.

As you continue forward, know that every small step matters, even the quiet moments. Trust the process, even on the days it feels difficult, and know that you are worthy of every good thing coming your way. Thank you for letting me be part of this journey, and thank you for choosing yourself. Here's to you—rising, reclaiming, and embracing the beautiful life ahead.

With all my heart,
Xo, Tia

 Tia Rochelle, a dynamic leader renowned as the Queen Mother of 5 and CEO of JahniSpot Concierge, epitomizes excellence in global concierge and event management. With over two decades of corporate expertise, Tia's unwavering dedication to empowering others transcends boundaries, inspiring individuals worldwide to reach their highest potential. As a devoted wife and mother, her commitment to fostering work-life harmony resonates deeply, while her innovative leadership has propelled her to the forefront of the industry. Tia's legacy is defined by her exceptional ability to cultivate meaningful relationships, orchestrate unparalleled events, and champion diversity and inclusion, solidifying her as a visionary force in both professional and personal spheres.

www.ingramcontent.com/pod-product-compliance
Lightning Source LLC
Chambersburg PA
CBHW051705090426
42736CB00013B/2550